lovestrong.
christina perri

This book was approved by Christina Perri

Piano/vocal arrangements by John Nicholas

Cherry Lane Music Company
Director of Publications/Project Editor: Mark Phillips

ISBN 978-1-60378-398-9

Visit our website at www.cherrylaneprint.com

christina perri

In July 2010, a struggling singer-songwriter and musician named Christina Perri had a life-changing moment when she was asked to perform a song she had written, a defiant break-up anthem called "Jar of Hearts," on the Fox show *So You Think You Can Dance*. The raw, emotional quality of her performance connected with viewers and catapulted the 24-year-old Philadelphia native into the public eye. "Jar of Hearts" went on to sell a million downloads and land Perri, who was then supporting herself as a café manager in Beverly Hills, a deal with Atlantic Records.

"Jar of Hearts" is just one of 12 brutally honest gems that Perri unveils on her debut album *lovestrong.*, a title she says reflects how her heart feels today. "I looked at the album as a whole piece and the two themes that stood out were love and strength," she says. "It really titled itself. Writing about love is just who I am. I've tried to write about other things, but ultimately this is what comes out of me."

Perri lays herself bare on *lovestrong.*, using her soaring, bittersweet voice and expressive piano playing to sketch out her stories. Some, like "Penguin" and "Arms," are happy and hopeful; some, like "Bang Bang Bang" and "Mine," are fun and playful; and others, like "The Lonely" and "Jar of Hearts," are downright wrenching. The common thread? "They're all songs I felt I needed to give away," she says. "I have been writing songs since I was 15, so I reached into my arsenal and picked the ones I felt others should hear. My intention for my music is pretty simple: I want to make people feel less broken and alone."

Perri sets *lovestrong.*'s hopeful tone with the second single, "Arms," a towering acoustic-guitar driven tune that builds to an urgent crescendo as its tale of the fight between the heart and the mind unfolds. "Your heart wants to be loved, but your head is telling you that you shouldn't be with that person," Perri says. "The song is about that struggle and finally giving in and letting love win."

It didn't really register how emotionally raw the album was going to be until Perri's 20th day in the recording studio. "In the vocal booth, I had to go back to the place and time that made me feel so vulnerable and rip open old wounds to sing each song, sometimes two songs in a day," she says. "Emotionally, it was the hardest 33 days of my life, but it was worth it because the result is that this album is 100 percent me. It's heartfelt, real, bold, honest, vulnerable, hopeful, strong, poetic, bluesy, gritty, pretty, and simple."

Produced by Joe Chiccareli (White Stripes, Tori Amos) and mixed by Michael Brauer (Coldplay, Regina Spektor), *lovestrong.* boasts a bold creative vision that is very much in keeping with Perri's spirited personality. A petite, tattooed ball of energy with an engaging smile, she has always embraced life to the fullest. Her adventures have included touring the world as an assistant to a rock band, spending a year at a prestigious university, producing popular music videos, making olive oil in Italy, and even serving as a fashionista barista in Beverly Hills.

On June 30, 2010, Perri got word that "Jar of Hearts" was going to air on *So You Think You Can Dance* as a backdrop to a memorable piece choreographed by Stacey Tookey. Viewers began downloading the song from iTunes in droves, sending "Jar of Hearts" into the Top 10 on the iTunes Pop chart and into the Top 15 on the Overall chart overnight. Impressed, *SYTYCD*'s producers invited Perri to play the song live on the show two weeks later. After Perri performed the song on July 15, "Jar of Hearts" landed at No. 25 on the *Billboard* Hot 100 chart, at No. 1 on Amazon's digital singles chart, and sold 200,000 downloads in three weeks. "While all of this was happening, I barely slept," Perri says, "because I was afraid it was just a dream; that I'd wake up and none of it would be real. One minute I didn't exist in the music world and the next minute I did."

Perri had actually been preparing for her big moment since she was a child. The daughter of hairdressers (whom she describes as "not musical, though my mom can whistle in many octaves"), Perri first sang in public at her Holy Communion at age six. Piano lessons began at age 8, but her piano teacher "fired" her (as she puts it) because "I would change the endings to the songs when I didn't like the way they were written." Eventually, Perri picked up a guitar and taught herself to play. She was in London working as a gofer for her brother's band Silvertide when she got word that she had been accepted to Philadelphia's prestigious University of the Arts with a sizeable scholarship. She attended for a year, but took a leave of absence to visit her father's extensive family in Italy. "I was 19 and I needed to soul search," she says. "I was still writing music, but I didn't know what I wanted to do with my life."

Still searching, Perri moved to Los Angeles with a suitcase and a guitar and recommitted herself to being a singer and a songwriter. She posted YouTube videos of herself performing her own songs, as well as covers, and shared her struggles in her uniquely humorous way. A video of one of her original compositions, "Tragedy" (which is included on *lovestrong.*), caught the attention of Bill Silva Management, who signed on to represent her. And so began Perri's charmed odyssey.

"Every day something happens that blows my mind," she says. "Being able to wake up and play music is more than I've ever dreamed my life could be. I'm looking forward to sharing my experiences, my hope, my strength, my guts, and my heart with the world."

Bluebird

Words and Music by
Christina Perri

Moderately slow, in 2

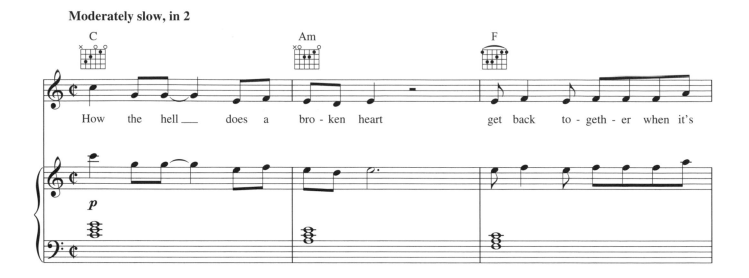

How the hell ___ does a bro-ken heart get back to-geth-er when it's

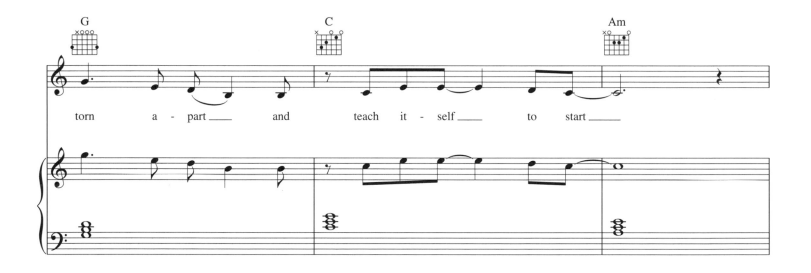

torn a - part ___ and teach it - self ___ to start ___

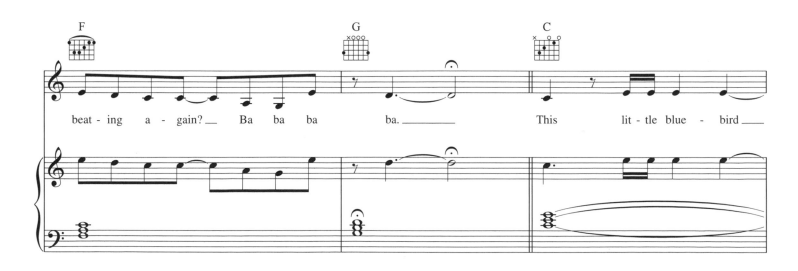

beat-ing a - gain? ___ Ba ba ba ba. ___ This lit - tle blue - bird ___

bet-ter than all _____ the rest. _____ I said

no, _____ you've got it all wrong. _____ If

he was some-thing spe - cial, I would-n't have this _____ song. _____

Don't you think _____ it was hard? _____ I did-n't e - ven say that you died. _____

But it would-n't have been ___ such ___ a lie, ___

'cause then I start -ed to cry. ___

How the hell ___ does a bro-ken heart get back to-geth-er when it's

torn a -part ___ and teach it -self ___ to start ___

beat - ing a - gain? __ Ba ba ba ba ba ba ba ba ba ba ba.

What if when __ she __ comes __ o - ver, I __

am in your arms, __ tak - ing all __ I want __ from you __ a - gain? __

Beat - ing a - gain.__ Ba ba ba ba.__

This lit - tle blue - bird __ don't come 'round here an - y - more. __

So I went look - ing for her, __ and I found __

you.

Arms

Words and Music by
Christina Perri and David Hodges

Moderately fast

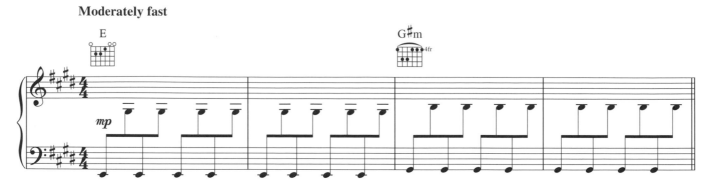

I nev-er thought ___ that ___ you ___ would be the

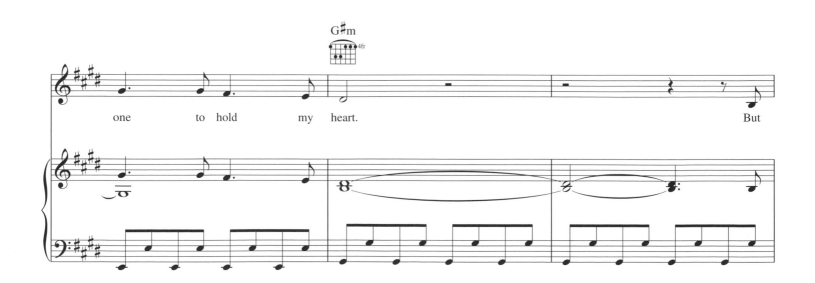

one to hold my heart. But

you came a - round ___ then you knocked me off the

ground _____ from the start.

You put your arms a - round me, and I be - lieve ___

___ that it's eas - i - er ___ for you ___ to let ___ me go. ___

The world is com - ing down ___ on me and

I can't find a rea - son to be loved.

I nev - er want to leave ___ you, but

Coda I

round me and I'm home _____ (home, _____ home). _____

I tried my / nev - er best to nev - er let you / o - pened up. I've nev - er

19

Bang Bang Bang

Words and Music by
Barrett Yeretsian, Christina Perri
and Drew Lawrence

man - y fights___ that I've fought___ and I've nev - er won.___

So I de - cid - ed that I___ should just give___ up on try - ing to

right your___ wrongs   And word on the street is that

she did to you what you did___ to___ me.___   Five,   four,

three, two, one.... Bang, bang, bang, boy, you're go - ing

down, down, down, boy, to the ground where you left my

heart to bleed. Bang, she shot you; kar - ma tastes so...

Bang, bang, bang, boy, you're go - ing down, down, down,

rules that we're mak - ing ex - cep - tions to. _____ But

how does it feel _____ to swim in your own _____ tears? _____

You lied and you lied and I died and I died and now

D.S. al Coda I

you know why. _____ Five, four, three, two, one... _____

cresc.

26

D.S. al Coda II

Bang, bang, _ bang, ____ boy, you're go - ing down, down, _ down, ____ boy, to the

ground where you left my heart to bleed. _ Bang, she shot you; kar - ma tastes _ so...

cresc.

Coda II

down _____ to the ground. ____

Ooh. _____

Distance

Words and Music by
Christina Perri and David Hodges

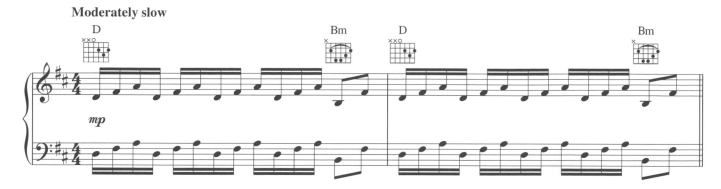

The sun is fill - ing up ___ the room and I can hear ___ you dream - ing. ___
Please don't stand ___ so close ___ to me; I'm hav - ing trou - ble breath - ing. ___

___ Do you feel ___ the way ___ I do right now?
I'm a - fraid ___ of what ___ you'll see right now.

you're   not   lis - 'ning. ___   How   long   till   we ___ call   this

love, ___   love,   love? _____

Jar of Hearts

Words and Music by
Barrett Yeretsian, Christina Perri
and Drew Lawrence

you lost the love I loved the most. I learned to live

half ____ a - live, and now you want me one more ____ time.

And who do you think you are, ____ run - ning 'round leav - ing

scars, _____ col - lect - ing your jar of hearts, ___ and tear - ing love a - part? _

To Coda

You're gon - na catch ___ a cold ___ from the ice in - side ___ your

soul. _____ So don't come back for me. Who do you think you are? ___

I hear you're ask - ing all a - round ___

if I am an - y - where to ___ be ___

Coda

It took so long just to feel al - right, re - mem - ber how to put back the light in my eyes. I wish I had missed the first time that we kissed 'cause you broke all your

38

from the ice in-side ___ your soul. ___ So don't come back for

me, ___ don't come back ___ at all. ___ And who do you think you're are, __

___ run-ning 'round ___ leav-ing scars, ___ col-lect-ing your jar of hearts, __

___ tear-ing love a-part? ___ You're gon-na catch ___ a cold __

Mine

Words and Music by
Christina Perri

grow. _____ A se-cret's safe _ be-hind _

_ a pret-ty _____ smile, _____ { and / but } it's

mine, mine, _ mine, _____ mine, mine, mine. __

To Coda

What's with all the late - night liq - uored

phone ___ calls? ___ I don't think ___ your lov-

D.S. al Coda

er likes ___ me at all. ___ A

Coda G A

What, what might you do ___

Moderately slow, in 2

Dm F/C B♭

to find out ___ why ___ I can't love ___ you, ___

44

Interlude

Words and Music by
Christina Perri and David Hodges

Penguin

Words and Music by
Christina Perri and John Anderson

*Guitarists: Use open D tuning (low to high: D-A-D-F♯-A-D) with capo at 2nd fret. Fret numbers to right of chord diagrams are relative to capo.

things he wants __ to learn, __ too; the hard-est parts __ you'll get __
love is strong __ and so __ true. His ar-row is aim - ing for __

__ through. And in the end, __ you'll have __ your best __ friend.
__ you. And he's the one __ that you __ were born __ to love.

Miles

Words and Music by
Christina Perri, David Hodges
and Greg Kurstin

I'm scared to - day, ___ more than I told you I was yes - ter - day. Give me a mo - ment to catch my breath and hold me ev - 'ry sec - ond left. ___ Proud of me; ___ that's _ the on - ly way I want _

you to be. ___ Look at me and love ___ what you ___ see. ___

I won't _ make it a - lone. I need some-thing to

hold.

Kiss me on __ my shoul - der ___ and tell me it's not o - ver. ___ I

prom - ise to al - ways come home _ to you. Re -

mind me that _ I'm old - er, _____ to be brave, smart, sweet and bold - er, _____ and

To Coda

don't give up on what we're try - 'n' to do.

Don't count the miles, _____ count the "I love _ you's."

prom - ise to come home to you. Re -

mind me that __ I'm old - er, _____ to be brave, smart, sweet and bold - er, _____ and

don't give up on what we're try - 'n' to do.

Don't count the miles, _____ count the "I love __ you's." __

The Lonely

Words and Music by
Christina Perri and David Hodges

Two a. - m., where do I be - gin?

Cry - ing off my face a - gain.

The si - lent sound of lone - li - ness

wants to fol - low me _____ to bed. I'm the ghost ___

___ of a girl ___ that I want ___ to be most. ___ I'm the

shell of a girl ___ that I used _____ to know well. _____

___ Danc - ing slow - ly in an emp - ty ___ room.

Sad Song

Words and Music by
Christina Perri

To-day I'm gon-na write a sad ___ song; ___ gon-na

I won-der what my mom and dad would say if I told them that I cry each day.

It's hard e-nough to live so far a-way.

D.S. al Coda

74

I can slip and fall and you won't ____ let ____ me go. ____ Just ____ let me know _____ that grow - ing up goes slow. And "I'm so sor - ry." ____

Tragedy

Words and Music by
Christina Perri and Nick Perri

you and me.___ But when it

comes down ___ to it, you nev - er made the most ___ of it.

Ooh, _____ so I cried, ___ cried, ___ cried _____

___ and now ___ I say good - bye._____

More Great Piano/Vocal Books

FROM CHERRY LANE

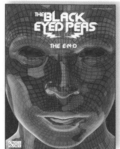

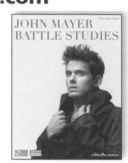

For a complete listing of Cherry Lane titles available, including contents listings, please visit our web site at
www.cherrylane.com

See your local music dealer or contact:

EXCLUSIVELY DISTRIBUTED BY

HAL•LEONARD CORPORATION

7777 W. BLUEMOUND RD. P.O. BOX 13819 MILWAUKEE, WI 53213

Prices, contents and availability subject to change without notice.

0811

More Big-Note & Easy Piano Books

For a complete listing of Cherry Lane titles available, including contents listings, please visit our web site at www.cherrylane.

CHOPIN FOR EASY PIANO
This special easy piano version features the composer's intricate melodies, harmonies and rhythms newly arranged so that virtually all pianists can experience the thrill of playing Chopin at the piano! Includes 20 favorites mazurkas, nocturnes, polonaises, preludes and waltzes.
_____ 02501483 Easy Piano...............$7.99

CLASSICAL CHRISTMAS
Easy solo arrangements of 30 wonderful holiday songs: Ave Maria • Dance of the Sugar Plum Fairy • Evening Prayer • Gesu Bambino • Hallelujah! • He Shall Feed His Flock • March of the Toys • O Come, All Ye Faithful • O Holy Night • Pastoral Symphony • Sheep May Safely Graze • Sinfonia • Waltz of the Flowers • and more.
_____ 02500112 Easy Piano Solo.......$9.95

BEST OF JOHN DENVER
A collection of 18 Denver classics, including: Leaving on a Jet Plane • Take Me Home, Country Roads • Rocky Mountain High • Follow Me • and more.
_____ 02505512 Easy Piano...............$9.95

JOHN DENVER ANTHOLOGY
Easy arrangements of 34 of the finest from this beloved artist. Includes: Annie's Song • Fly Away • Follow Me • Grandma's Feather Bed • Leaving on a Jet Plane • Perhaps Love • Rocky Mountain High • Sunshine on My Shoulders • Take Me Home, Country Roads • Thank God I'm a Country Boy • and many more.
_____ 02501366 Easy Piano.............$19.99

EASY BROADWAY SHOWSTOPPERS
Easy piano arrangements of 16 traditional and new Broadway standards, including: "Impossible Dream" from *Man of La Mancha* • "Unusual Way" from *Nine* • "This Is the Moment" from *Jekyll & Hyde* • many more.
_____ 02505517 Easy Piano.............$12.95

A FAMILY CHRISTMAS AROUND THE PIANO
25 songs for hours of family fun, including: Away in a Manger • Deck the Hall • The First Noel • God Rest Ye Merry, Gentlemen • Hark! the Herald Angels Sing • Jingle Bells • Jolly Old St. Nicholas • Joy to the World • O Little Town of Bethlehem • Silent Night, Holy Night • The Twelve Days of Christmas • and more.
_____ 02500398 Easy Piano...............$8.99

FAVORITE CELTIC SONGS FOR EASY PIANO
Easy arrangements of 40 Celtic classics, including: The Ash Grove • The Bluebells of Scotland • A Bunch of Thyme • Danny Boy • Finnegan's Wake • I'll Tell Me Ma • Loch Lomond • My Wild Irish Rose • The Rose of Tralee • and more!
_____ 02501306 Easy Piano.............$12.99

FAVORITE POP BALLADS
This new collection features 35 beloved ballads, including: Breathe (2 AM) • Faithfully • Leaving on a Jet Plane • Open Arms • Ordinary People • Summer Breeze • These Eyes • Truly • You've Got a Friend • and more.
_____ 02501005 Easy Piano.............$15.99

HOLY CHRISTMAS CAROLS COLORING BOOK
A terrific songbook with 7 sacred carols and lots of coloring pages for the young pianist. Songs include: Angels We Have Heard on High • The First Noel • Hark! The Herald Angels Sing • It Came upon a Midnight Clear • O Come All Ye Faithful • O Little Town of Bethlehem • Silent Night.
_____ 02500277 Five-Finger Piano $6.95

JEKYLL & HYDE – VOCAL SELECTIONS
Ten songs from the Wildhorn/Bricusse Broadway smash, arranged for big-note: In His Eyes • It's a Dangerous Game • Lost in the Darkness • A New Life • No One Knows Who I Am • Once Upon a Dream • Someone Like You • Sympathy, Tenderness • Take Me as I Am • This Is the Moment.
_____ 02500023 Big-Note Piano........$9.95

JACK JOHNSON ANTHOLOGY
Easy arrangements of 27 of the best from this Hawaiian singer/songwriter, including: Better Together • Breakdown • Flake • Fortunate Fool • Good People • Sitting, Waiting, Wishing • Taylor • and more.
_____ 02501313 Easy Piano.............$19.99

JUST FOR KIDS – *NOT!* CHRISTMAS SONGS
This unique collection of 14 Christmas favorites is fun for the whole family! Kids can play the full-sounding big-note solos alone, or with their parents (or teachers) playing accompaniment for the thrill of four-hand piano! Includes: Deck the Halls • Jingle Bells • Silent Night • What Child Is This? • and more.
_____ 02505510 Big-Note Piano $8.95

JUST FOR KIDS – *NOT!* CLASSICS
Features big-note arrangements of classical masterpieces, plus optional accompaniment for adults. Songs: Air on the G String • Dance of the Sugar Plum Fairy • Für Elise • Jesu, Joy of Man's Desiring • Ode to Joy • Pomp and Circumstance • The Sorcerer's Apprentice • William Tell Overture • and more!
_____ 02505513 Classics $7.95
_____ 02500301 More Classics..........$8.95

JUST FOR KIDS – *NOT!* FUN SONGS
Fun favorites for kids everywhere in big-note arrangements for piano, including: Bingo • Eensy Weensy Spider • Farmer in the Dell • Jingle Bells • London Bridge • Pop Goes the Weasel • Puff the Magic Dragon • Skip to My Lou • Twinkle, Twinkle Little Star • and more!
_____ 02505523 Fun Songs $7.95

JUST FOR KIDS – *NOT!* TV THEMES & MOVIE SONGS
Entice the kids to the piano with this delightful collection of songs and themes from movies and TV. These big-note arrangements include themes from The Brady Bunch and The Addams Family, as well as Do-Re-Mi (The Sound of Music), theme from Beetlejuice (Day-O) and Puff the Magic Dragon. Each song includes an accompaniment part for teacher or adult so that the kids can experience the joy of four-hand playing as well! Plus performance tips.
_____ 02505507 TV Themes & Movie
      Songs.......................$9.95
_____ 02500304 More TV Themes & Movie
      Songs.......................$9.95

MERRY CHRISTMAS, EVERYONE
Over 20 contemporary and classic all-time holiday favorites arranged for big-note piano or easy piano. Includes: Away in a Manger • Christmas Like a Lullaby • The First Noel • Joy to the World • The Marvelous Toy • and more.
_____ 02505600 Big-Note Piano........$9.95

POKEMON 2 B.A. MASTER
This great songbook features easy piano arrangements of 13 tunes from the hit TV series: 2.B.A. Master • Double Trouble (Team Rocket) • Everything Changes • Misty's Song • My Best Friends • Pokémon (Dance Mix) • Pokémon Theme • PokéRAP • The Time Has Come (Pikachu's Goodbye) • Together, Forever • Viridian City • What Kind of Pokémon Are You? • You Can Do It (If You Really Try). Includes a full-color, 8-page pull-out section featuring characters and scenes from this super hot show.
_____ 02500145 Easy Piano.............$12.95

POP/ROCK LOVE SONGS
Easy arrangements of 18 romatic favorites, including: Always • Bed of Roses • Butterfly Kisses • Follow Me • From This Moment On • Hard Habit to Break • Leaving on a Jet Plane • When You Say Nothing at All • more.
_____ 02500151 Easy Piano.............$10.95

POPULAR CHRISTMAS CAROLS COLORING BOOK
Kids are sure to love this fun holiday songbook! It features five-finger piano arrangements of seven Christmas classics, complete with coloring pages throughout! Songs include: Deck the Hall • Good King Wenceslas • Jingle Bells • Jolly Old St. Nicholas • O Christmas Tree • Up on the Housetop • We Wish You a Merry Christmas.
_____ 02500276 Five-Finger Piano $6.95

PUFF THE MAGIC DRAGON & 54 OTHER ALL-TIME CHILDREN'S FAVORITESONGS
55 timeless songs enjoyed by generations of kids, and sure to be favorites for years to come. Songs include: A-Tisket A-Tasket • Alouette • Eensy Weensy Spider • The Farmer in the Dell • I've Been Working on the Railroad • If You're Happy and You Know It • Joy to the World • Michael Finnegan • Oh Where, Oh Where Has My Little Dog Gone • Silent Night • Skip to My Lou • This Old Man • and many more.
_____ 02500017 Big-Note Piano $12.95

See your local music dealer or contact:

EXCLUSIVELY DISTRIBUTED BY
HAL•LEONARD®
7777 W. BLUEMOUND RD. P.O. BOX 13819 MILWAUKEE, WI 53213

Prices, contents, and availability subject to change without notice.

0811

SUPPLY THE DEMAND
WITH THE MOST REQUESTED SERIES FROM

cherry lane
music company

THE MOST REQUESTED ACOUSTIC SONGS

Featuring pop, rock, country, and more, this fun collection includes favorite tunes such as: American Pie • Better Together • Black Water • The Boxer • Burn One Down • Cat's in the Cradle • Crash into Me • Crazy Little Thing Called Love • Free Fallin' • Friend of the Devil • I Walk the Line • I've Just Seen a Face • Landslide • More Than Words • Patience • Redemption Song • Summer Breeze • To Be with You • Toes • Wish You Were Here • and many more.

00001518 P/V/G $19.99

THE MOST REQUESTED BROADWAY SONGS

60 tunes from the Great White Way, including: And I'm Telling You I'm Not Going • Aquarius • Beauty and the Beast • Can You Feel the Love Tonight • Corner of the Sky • Getting to Know You • Everything's Coming Up Roses • I Enjoy Being a Girl • It's Delovely • Mack the Knife • Mame • New York, New York • Oh, What a Beautiful Mornin' • On My Own • Part of Your World • People • Seasons of Love • Stop the World I Want to Get Off • The Impossible Dream • Til There Was You • Tomorrow • What I Did for Love • and more.

00001557 P/V/G $19.99

THE MOST REQUESTED CHRISTMAS SONGS

This giant collection features nearly 70 holiday classics, from traditional carols to modern Christmas hits: Blue Christmas • The Christmas Song (Chestnuts Roasting on an Open Fire) • Christmas Time Is Here • Deck the Hall • Feliz Navidad • Grandma Got Run over by a Reindeer • Have Yourself a Merry Little Christmas • I'll Be Home for Christmas • Jingle Bells • Little Saint Nick • The Most Wonderful Time of the Year • Nuttin' for Christmas • Rudolph the Red-Nosed Reindeer • Silent Night • The Twelve Days of Christmas • Wonderful Christmastime • and more.

00001563 P/V/G $19.99

THE MOST REQUESTED CLASSIC ROCK SONGS

Turn up the volume for this fun collection of 60 classic rock tunes. Songs include: Africa • Bang a Gong (Get It On) • Don't Stop Believin' • Feelin' Alright • Hello, It's Me • A Horse with No Name • I've Seen All Good People • Layla • The Letter • Life in the Fast Lane • Maybe I'm Amazed • Money • Only the Good Die Young • Peace of Mind • Rikki Don't Lose That Number • Sister Christian • Small Town • Space Oddity • Tiny Dancer • Walk Away Renee • We Are the Champions • and more!

02501632 P/V/G $19.99

THE MOST REQUESTED PARTY SONGS

This good time collection includes hits heard at weddings and bar mitzvahs across the U.S.A, such as: Another One Bites the Dust • Bang the Drum All Day • Brown Eyed Girl • Celebration • Dancing Queen • Electric Slide • Get down Tonight • Girls Just Want to Have Fun • Hava Nagila (Let's Be Happy) • Hot Hot Hot • I Gotta Feeling • In Heaven There Is No Beer • Limbo Rock • The Loco-Motion • 1999 • Shout • Twist and Shout • Y.M.C.A. • and many more.

00001576 P/V/G $19.99

THE MOST REQUESTED WEDDING SONGS

50 songs perfect for the big day of "I Do"'s, including: Because You Loved Me • Butterfly Kisses • Celebration • Father and Daughter • From This Moment On • Have I Told You Lately • How Sweet It Is (To Be Loved by You) • Hungry Eyes • I Gotta Feeling • I Will Always Love You • In My Life • Isn't She Lovely • Last Dance • Let's Get It On • Love and Marriage • My Girl • Still the One • Sunrise, Sunset • Through the Years • Unforgettable • The Way You Look Tonight • We Are Family • The Wind Beneath My Wings • Wonderful Tonight • Y.M.C.A. • You're Still the One • and more.

02501750 P/V/G $19.99

SEE YOUR LOCAL MUSIC DEALER OR CONTACT:

cherry lane
music company

EXCLUSIVELY DISTRIBUTED BY
HAL•LEONARD CORPORATION
7777 W. BLUEMOUND RD. P.O. BOX 13819 MILWAUKEE, WI 53213

PRICES, CONTENT, AND AVAILABILITY SUBJECT TO CHANGE WITHOUT NOTICE.

1111